EXCERPTS FROM

THE TURIN SHROUD:

PHYSICAL EVIDENCE *OF LIFE AFTER DEATH?*

MARK NIYR

Bookstand Publishing

www.bookstandpublishing.com

Published by
Bookstand Publishing
Pasadena, CA 91101
4822_19

ISBN 978-1-63498-998-5

LICENSING PERMISSIONS
FOR USE OF THIS WORK

CONTENTS

Chapter 1

SCIENTIFIC INVESTIGATION OF
THE SHROUD

One evening I was watching the news on television. They reported that passenger airliner Germanwings Flight U4 9525 from Barcelona, Spain to Duesseldorf, Germany had crashed killing all 150 people on board. The co-pilot had planned it all as a personal suicide. The flight had climbed to an altitude of 38,000 ft (11,600m). Once the pilot left the cockpit to visit the restroom, the co-pilot disabled the pilot's code which unlocks the cockpit door. He then began the descent at a rate of 3-4,000 feet per minute. As heard from the surviving cockpit voice recorder, the pilot returned and is heard yelling, then pounding on the door, and then trying to break into the cockpit with an axe retrieved by the crew. Passengers who became aware of what was going on could be heard screaming in the background. The television news broadcast played the final audio moments from the cockpit voice recorder. During those final moments, the aircraft must have broken through the obscurity of cloud cover just before its crash into the French Alps. The passengers could now see out the windows the approaching impact. All at once, there was an instantaneous, bloodcurdling, loud burst of screams. I heard this with my own ears during the newscast. It was traumatic. It was shocking. I will never forget it.[a]

People often live day to day focused on the affairs of their lives—but paying little, if any, serious attention about the possibility of life after death?

---

[a] BBC, "Germanwings Crash: What Happened in the Final 30 Minutes," March 23, 2017, https://www.bbc.com/news/world-europe-32072218; The New York Times, "Germanwings Crash: How the Lock on the Cockpit Door Works," March 26, 2015; Clark, Nicola; Bilefsky, Dan, "Germanwings Pilot Was Locked Out of Cockpit Before Crash in France," March 26, 2015.

Is it possible there might be *physical evidence* of life after death? *Physical evidence?* What if scientists worldwide could examine, research, and test such physical evidence from numerous scientific perspectives? What if some scientists hoped to disprove it, while others just wanted to investigate the evidence? What if international scientists could lavish their efforts over many decades in order to meticulously pursue this research? Would you like to review their scientific findings so you could draw your own conclusion?

What is the most scientifically studied relic in history? Some people might surmise it would be the Rosetta Stone (which unlocked the interpretation of Egyptian hieroglyphs). However, the answer is unquestionably the Shroud of Turin. Hundreds of thousands of scientific hours of analysis, research, and testing have been devoted to the Shroud. In the process, international scientists have employed some of the most sophisticated scientific equipment and technology in the world, involving such prestigious institutions as (to name a few) Los Alamos Scientific Laboratory, Jet Propulsion Laboratory, U.S. Air Force, Sandia Laboratory, Zurich Criminal Police, and universities such as Harvard, Yale, Cambridge, and Oxford. Never before had such an impressive body of scientists of the highest caliber, from such a diverse range of scientific disciplines and professional fields, from regions throughout the world, brought together such extensive research to bear on a relic of antiquity. Their research (published in numerous books, peer-reviewed scientific journals, academic, and professional publications throughout the world) is extensive and compelling.

> **"The Shroud of Turin is the single, most studied artifact in human history"** — *Journal of Research of the National Institute of Standards and Technology,* **U.S. Department of Commerce.** [b]

---

[b] Lloyd A. Currie, "The Remarkable Metrological History of Radiocarbon Dating [II], *Journal of Research of the National Institute of Standards and Technology* 109, no. 2 (March-April 2004): 185-217, https://nvlpubs.nist.gov/nistpubs/jres/109/2/j92cur.pdf ; P.

Have you ever wondered what might have been the result if modern scientists had been given an opportunity to examine one of the acclaimed miracles of Christ? The Shroud of Turin may provide just such an opportunity. Will it pass the scientific test?

This book is only intended as an introductory abridged version of the complete book entitled *The Turin Shroud: Physical Evidence of Life After Death? (With Insights from a Jewish Perspective)*. If this subject interest the reader, he or she is encouraged to purchase the complete book. It reviews far more extensive and compelling discoveries concerning the Shroud of Turin, and documents every fact with hundreds of reference notes. Likewise, for readers who have scriptural concerns about the Shroud, they would most likely find answers to their questions in Chapter 23 of the complete book.

Congregational leaders should be encouraged to purchase the complete book so they may read it to their congregations from a series of lectures a few chapters at a time. (There is far too much science and important information for a non-science public speaker to recite this from memory, or from lecture notes. However, it would be quite complimentary for the speaker to interject various comments while traversing through the text.) This topic is important for congregational leaders to share with their people because it is potentially ***the only surviving miracle from Christ left behind after 2,000 years.*** Our generation **deserves** a chance to personally witness this (and **draw our own conclusions**)! The annual anniversary of the resurrection would be an ideal time to review this.

Damon, D. J. Donahue, B. H. Gore, A. L. Hatheway, A. J. T. Jull, T. W. Linick, P. J. Sercel, L. J. Toolin, C. R. Bronk, E. T. Hall, R. E. M. Hedges, R. Housley, I. A. Law, C. Perry, G. Bonani, S. Trumbore, W. Wölfli, J. C. Ambers, S. G. E. Bowman, M. N. Leese, and M. S. Tite, "Radiocarbon dating of the Shroud of Turin," *Nature* **337,** (1989), 611-615.

Individual readers may also provide a service to their own place of worship by recommending that their congregational leaders offer a series of lectured readings from the chapters of the complete book.

Chapter 2

WHAT IS THE SHROUD OF TURIN?

The Shroud of Turin is an ancient linen cloth (14 feet 3 inches long by 3 feet 7 inches wide, or 4.34 m x 1.10 m) which is purported to be the burial cloth that wrapped the body of Christ in the tomb. It bears a life-size full body image of a crucified victim which perfectly matches the biblical description of the crucified Nazarene—including all the variety of wounds described in the gospels. *Could the Shroud (with this image) be a physical by-product of the resurrection of Christ—capturing that moment from an event of 2,000 years ago? Could it be physical evidence of life after death?*

Your Decision: You Make the Call

(a) Is the image on the Shroud an accident of nature?

(b) Is the image an artistic forgery: a hoax?

(c) Or, is the image authentic—a miracle left behind from the historical Christ, some 2,000 years ago? *You* decide for yourself.

Chapter 3

A BRIEF HISTORY OF THE SHROUD

If the Shroud is the historical burial cloth of the crucified Christ, then the Shroud's first recorded history took place in Jerusalem, such as recorded in the Gospel of Mark:

> He [*Yosef* / Joseph from *Ramatayim* / Arimathea] bought a linen cloth, took him [Christ] down [from the cross], **wrapped him in the linen cloth**, and laid him in a tomb which had been cut out of a rock. He rolled a stone against the door of the tomb (Mark 15:46, MW, emphasis added).

- The first extra-biblical account of the shroud's history is found from ancient Syriac manuscripts. They cite that the Shroud was brought to the city of Edessa (modern day Urfa, Turkey) during the first century.

- Persecutions led to the Shroud being hidden away until it was later rediscovered in a niche within the top of Edessa's city gate (year 525).

- The Shroud was moved from Edessa to Constantinople (modern day Istanbul, Turkey) during year 943.

- The French 4th crusade besieged Constantinople on occasions between 1203 and 1204. At that point the Shroud disappeared.

- The next documented history of the Shroud occurred in the village of Lirey, France during the 1300s. At that time there were public expositions of the Shroud in Lirey, France (circa 1357 and 1389-1390), which drew large crowds of pilgrims from various nations who could purchase souvenir pilgrim badge medallions (made of tin and lead) skillfully depicting the full Shroud with impressive details, including its unique flow of blood trails, and a very complex, expensive weave pattern of the linen cloth on the back of the medallions.

A couple of these pilgrim souvenir medallions from the Lirey expositions of the Shroud still exist today. One is kept at the Cluny Museum in Paris, France. All this is highly significant because the Lirey Medallion displays an embossed depictment of the *entire* shroud. *It is the earliest historical portrayal of the Shroud that offers a detailed visual illustration of the complete Shroud. It demonstrates what the Shroud looked like at that time (during the 1300s)—and it is an unmistakable replica of the Shroud which today resides in Turin, Italy.* On the lower right corner of the Lirey Medallion, it presents three shields within a shield which was the "coat of arms" symbol of a family owner of the Shroud (Geoffrey I de Charny, lord of Lirey, France) who had died on the battlefield of Poitiers on September 19, 1356. **Thus, for the first time in recorded history we have a** *full visual confirmation* **that the Shroud (which today resides in Turin, Italy) is the very same Shroud that existed in Lirey, France during the 1300s.**

Fig. 1.

Descent from the Cross with the Shroud of Turin painted by artist Giulio Clovio 1498-1578

Above: Angels hold a painted portrayal of the Shroud.
Below: Illustrates how the Shroud was wrapped around the body.

Fig. 2.

Photo of the Cluny Pilgrim Medallion (Lirey Pilgrim Medallion)
by Arthor Forgeais (1822-1878)
published year 1865 in France

This was a souvenir purchased by visitors to the Shroud expositions displayed in Lirey, France during the 1300s. It is the earliest dated visual depictment of the *entire* Shroud. ***It confirms that the Shroud of the 1300s was unmistakably the same Shroud which today resides in Turin, Italy.*** This medallion is now in possession of the Cluny Museum in Paris, France. The medallion illustrates two men at the top holding the Shroud at an exposition. (Unfortunately, both of their heads have been broken off from the medallion.) On the medallion's lower right corner, it displays three shields within a shield which was the coat of arms symbol of a family owner of the Shroud Geoffrey I de Charny who had died on the battlefield of Poitiers on September 19, 1356. The medallion is proof that the Turin Shroud existed during the 1300s.

Chapter 4

THE IMAGE CHARACTERISTICS:
LIKE A PHOTOGRAPHIC NEGATIVE?

To the natural eye (when viewed in person), the image on the Shroud appears like a faint blur. Its form displays as though someone had applied a wet, blunt sponge to the cloth with some light coloring to fashion its features. Eventually, in 1898, Italian photographer Secondo Pia took the first-ever photograph of the Shroud. He did not expect that his photo would look different from the faint, blurry image he had examined while surveying the cloth. Instead of the expected spongy, blurry image, the developing negative plate resolved into a lifelike, vivid, sharply focused, positive photographic-like depiction! This meant that the image on the Shroud somehow bore characteristics like a photographic *negative*, which upon being photographed, produced a *positive-like* photographic result on the *negative* plate (instead of the expected negative image on the negative plate). How could that be? The confirmed existence of the Turin Shroud dates back to at least the 1300s, whereas photography and the concept of photonegativity would not be invented until more than 400 years later (the early 1800s). French physicist Joseph Nicephor Niepce made the world's first photo-like negative image on paper in 1816, and the first known photograph in 1826. When the first photograph of the Shroud was made in 1898, what previously had been a faint, blurry, spongy appearance on the Shroud now leaped out from the photographic negative with sharply defined focus, with precise depth shadowing, reversed light/dark contrast, and reversed left/right positioning—precisely what results when a negative is transformed into a positive with photography. New details that had previously been invisible to the natural eye now became visible on the photographic negative.

How could a medieval craftsman from the 1300s produce a *photo-like* negative image more than *400 years before the invention of photography and photo-negativity*? How could the artist include details that would remain invisible to the naked eye for five centuries until the invention of photography and the Shroud's first photograph in 1898? The medieval forger would have no way to see this transformation effect. No cameras would be available for the forger to view this photographic effect until centuries later. Take a moment to look over the photo on the front cover of this book. Suppose you were the medieval artist. When you examine the photo on the cover, if you had no concept of photography, would you ever imagine that the blurry view of the Shroud seen by the naked eye (on the left side of the front book cover) would transform itself into the photographic, life-like image (displayed on the right side of the book cover photo) once it was revealed centuries later by the invention of photography?

Applying inductive logic pertaining to this photographic feature, what is your appraisal? What seems most plausible to you? (1) Does this appear to be an accident of nature? Or (2), is this most likely the work of a medieval forger from the 1300s? Or (3), does this photo-like negative image more likely point to an authentic relic? What is your honest appraisal regarding this? (Please stop to decide your evaluation for just this one particular aspect of the Shroud before reading further. You will be invited to give your opinion on other features about the Shroud as we continue.)

Note: there are no other examples in history of a burial cloth revealing any image. Throughout the centuries, archeologists have uncovered thousands of ancient burial cloths. But none of them have left any sort of image. Scientists have not considered the "accident by nature" scenario as a credible option. They have only treated two alternatives as plausible for their research: (1) either the image is the result of an artistic forgery, or (2) the Shroud's image is an authentic relic which baffles scientific explanation.

See the front book cover to view the face. It juxtaposes the view as seen from the natural eye (L) versus the view from the photo negative (R).

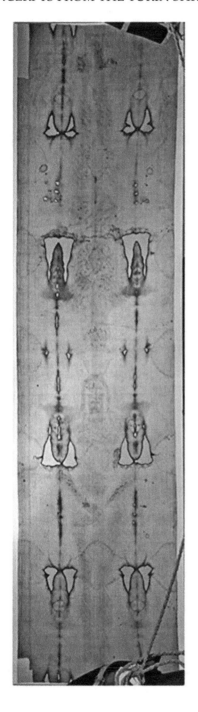

Fig. 3.

Full image of the Shroud as seen by the natural eye.

There are repair patches, scorch marks, and water stains that resulted centuries ago when fires broke out.

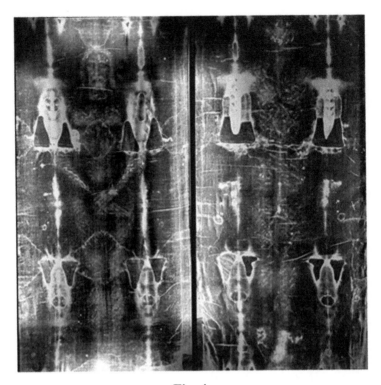

Fig. 4.

Ventral (front) and dorsal (back) photographic, life-like Shroud image.

How could a medieval forger anticipate that this blurry shroud image seen by the natural eye (fig. 3) would transform into the sharply resolved focus of this life-like, photo-like image? The artist would have no cameras to see this transformation effect. Photography would not be invented until 500 years later. Compare this sharp photo image versus the blurry view from the natural eye when seen in person (cf., book cover and fig. 3). Notice the negative image (white) blood on the wrist area from the nail wounds, and the corresponding (white) rivulets of blood trails along the forearms. Observe the (white) blood on the head (indicative of the crown of thorns). Negative image (white) blood is also evident from the nail spike through the feet. White on the right side of the chest is blood from a pierce wound to the ribs. Whipped scourge marks appear over the entire torso. All these wounds match the gospel record. Various abnormal features are from repair patches, scorch marks, and water stains that resulted centuries ago when fires broke out.

Chapter 5

A THREE-DIMENSIONAL IMAGE?

Once technology developed to the point of being able to produce simulated three-dimensional elevations from brightness maps with a VP-8 Image Analyzer, physicist John Jackson and Bill Mottern (an image specialist at Sandia Laboratory, the renowned atomic weapons facility) made arrangements for a test to be made at Sandia Laboratory to observe what would happen if the Shroud's image was processed by a VP-8 Image Analyzer. They were stunned by the result: *The Shroud gave off a correctly proportioned **three-dimensional** display of its image!* When a normal photograph is processed by the VP-8 Image Analyzer, the image is collapsed and distorted. Yet, when viewing the Shroud from the Image Analyzer, it rendered a striking 3D display, such that from the screen monitor they could explore the body's three-dimensional form and follow it as though traversing a range of mountains from a moving helicopter. A flat two-dimensional Shroud cloth had conferred this three-dimensionally encoded information. How could that be?

Indeed, it is the scientists that truly recognize how "astonishing" and "mind-blowing" these discoveries were—far more than the average person who is a non-scientist. For example, with a normal photograph of the front of a face, the view is restricted to that frontal perspective. But with the Shroud's 3D image, there is not only the frontal view, but the face may also be observed from either side-to-side facial profiles in 3D—such as viewing from the left side profile and then over across to the right-side profile of the face. It is mind-boggling to think that a flat two-dimensional cloth could confer a three-dimensional image.

Engineer Peter Schumacher (who pioneered the production and delivery of the VP-8 Image Analyzer) wrote a paper delivered at the

Shroud of Turin International Research Conference in Richmond, Virginia, regarding his initial encounter with this:

> A "true-three-dimensional image" appeared on the monitor. . . . The nose ramped in relief. The facial features were contoured properly. Body shapes of the arms, legs, and chest, had the basic human form. This result from the VP-8 had never occurred with any of the images I had studied, nor had I heard of it happening during any image studies done by others.
>
> I had never heard of the Shroud of Turin before that moment. I had no idea what I was looking at. However, the results are unlike anything I have processed through the VP-8 Analyzer, before or since. Only the Shroud of Turin has produced these results from a VP-8 Image Analyzer isometric projection study.[c]

Schumacher added:

> One must consider how and why an artist would embed three-dimensional information in the grey shading of an image. In fact, no means of viewing this property of the image would be available for at least 650 years after it was done. One would have to ask . . . "Why isn't this result obtained in the analysis of other works? . . . Why would the artist make only one such work requiring such special skills and talent, and not pass the technique along to others? How could the artist control the quality of the work when the artist could not "see" grey scale as elevation? . . .
>
> The VP-8 Image Analyzer's isometric display is a "dumb" process. That means it does one process on whatever "data" is sent to it. . . . Like a photographic negative, the process is not "involved" in the result. It is simply photons in and voltage out. The Shroud image

---

[c] Quotation with permission from Peter M. Schumacher, "Photogrammetric Responses from The Shroud of Turin," 1999, *Shroud of Turin Website*, http://www.shroud.com/pdfs/schumchr.pdf .

induces the three-dimensional result. It is the only image known to induce this result.[d]

Not only the front (ventral) side of the body is three-dimensional, but also the back (dorsal) side of the body. What is found on the dorsal (back) side is of particular significance. The buttocks are not flattened by gravity from the weight of the body. They are fully round — defying gravity. This is due to the body's stiffened, ridged state of rigor mortis. Rigor mortis can only last for a limited time — during the first two or three days after death. This duration of rigor mortis precisely correlates with the time frame reported between the burial and resurrection of Christ. Such brief duration (two or three days) would not have left much time for an image to develop on the cloth.

Bear in mind: photographs do not render three-dimensional information. Photographs only convey light, darkness and color. Here with the Shroud, we have a two-dimensional flat cloth that is embedded with three-dimensional encodement (the "grey scale") which communicates the distance between the cloth and the body at every *pin point* location between the body and the Shroud. Unlike a photograph, the Shroud's 3D image provides left, center, and right profiles of the head as well as with the front and back of the entire body when the "grey scale" is decoded.

Now imagine a craftsman from the 1300s trying to encode this life-size three-dimensional image upon the flat two-dimensional cloth. He could not see any result from his efforts to construct this 3D effect until *six centuries later* (when modern science would finally develop the technology to translate the encodement into its three-dimensional depth).

---

[d] Ibid. Quotation with permission from Peter M. Schumacher.

Your opinion: Is the 3D result most likely a product fabricated by a medieval artist from the 1300s? Or, is this evidence most indicative of an authentic relic? You decide.

INSTRUCTIONS: HOW TO VIEW THE 3D SHROUD IMAGE

By year 2006, the first 3D hologram of the Shroud image was produced. It was later filmed into a video offering a scan across the 3D image from side-to-side profiles. This was accomplished by Dr. Petrus Soons and Bernardo Galmarini in conjunction with Dutch Holographic Laboratory in the Netherlands. **Readers are encouraged to view the videos of the three-dimensional image where they may observe the body from side-to-side profiles. The visual results are all the more striking when viewed with 3D glasses.**[e] Keep in mind that the actual image is life-size (not small like your computer screen). There are many videos of the Shroud, **but only the two videos listed below are the exclusive and genuine 3D videos of the Shroud.** They required special technical holographic processing in order to decode the 3D "grey scale" encodement embedded within the flat Shroud cloth. **To watch the 3D videos, go to any website; then from that website, type in one of the two URL addresses listed below into the address bar. Then press the enter key. (If the URL bar responds offering several selections, you may need to try each, one at a time, to find the correct video.) To confirm that you found the correct video, verify that the video displays the "title, date, and time" listed here below.**

https://www.youtube.com/watch?v=G9K3yw0oKr4
("**PICTURES OF JESUS**" – Feb 21 2011 – Time **0:30**)

https://www.youtube.com/watch?v=y_of-ou4BFs
("**THE SHROUD OF TURIN 3D HOLOGRAM**" – Mar 19 2013 – Time 1:27)

---

[e] 3D glasses may be purchased at a low price from Amazon.com.

Once you confirm that you found the correct video, save it to your Favorites or Bookmark it on your PC for future quick and easy access.

I recommend watching the videos in "theater mode" by clicking that option in the lower right corner. If you have 3D glasses, position your eyes about 4 feet away from your computer screen. Darken your room to watch the video. To see it again, simply click the "REPLAY" button at the lower left corner of the video. Also try this: when you click the "REPLAY" button on the lower left corner, then immediately pause the video at the beginning. While in "pause mode," click your cursor every half inch along the video timeline to compare the paused profiles from different angle perspectivess. If you have 3D glasses, view the "paused" video image without the 3D glasses, and then pull the 3D glasses down over your eyes to see the paused image transform into its full 3D effect. However, the second video only displays full 3D effect for the horizontal body image (time 1:07). But when you lift the 3D glasses on and off your eyes for that horizontal body image, then the body image protrudes three-dimensionally outward beyond your flat computer screen. While watching the videos, keep in mind that you are seeing this from a **flat** 2D burial cloth which renders this 3D effect.

These 3D hologram images were decoded from the 3D ("grey scale") encodement embedded within the linen fibers of the flat 2D Shroud cloth. The "grey scale" from the Shroud fibers conveyed the distance information between each pinpoint location of the body to its corresponding pinpoint location on Shroud.

3D holography was not invented until 1947 when Dennis Gabor originated its concept and eventually won the Nobel Prize for Physics for his invention of the holographic method in 1971 (*six hundred years after any alleged medieval Shroud craftsman*).

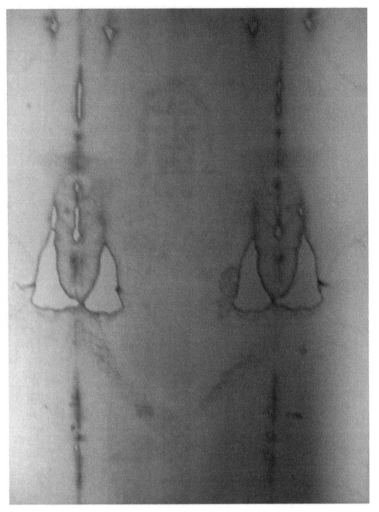

Fig. 5.

Ventral (upper front) image of the Shroud as seen in person by the natural eye.

This is the view of the Shroud as seen by the natural eye in person. It appears faint and blurry as though the image was made by dipping a blunt sponge to apply some light-colored substance. Can you decipher from this natural eye point of view that the Shroud cloth is embedded with three-dimensional encodement? If not, then how could an alleged medieval craftsman from the 1300s create and perceive any effect of an embedded three-dimensional code?

Chapter 6

WHAT MADE THE IMAGE ON THE SHROUD?

WHY DIDN'T THE DISCIPLES REPORT FINDING AN IMAGE ON THE SHROUD?

Based on scientific research of the Turin Shroud, it would be expected that no image would have been visible on the Shroud for many years until the Shroud began to age and yellow over time. The image was not burnt or scorched on the Shroud, nor is there any substance on the Shroud (such as paint or pigmentation) that makes its image. If it had been, then the image would have immediately appeared. Rather, evidence from the Shroud is conclusive that, where its image exists, it is due exclusively to *molecular changes to its image fibers* which gradually caused the image fibers to *yellow and darken faster over time* than the overall Shroud cloth (like an old newspaper under the sun). According to the Historically Consistent Hypothesis, the likely source inducing the molecular change was proton and alpha particle radiation acquired when the Shroud collapsed by gravity and was sucked into the vacuum and residual proton and alpha particle radiation of the body when the body transferred into an alternate dimensionality. Such radiation would break apart many of the molecular bonds of the image fibers causing carbon and oxygen atoms to double-bond with each other. This molecular change resulted in *conjugated carbonyl (double-bonded) groups* within the molecular structure of the cellulose fibers of the Shroud image. Subsequent air and sunlight exposure would gradually induce oxidized, dehydrated cellulose, causing the image fibers to *yellow and darken faster than the non image fibers of the cloth over time—slowly revealing its image as the cloth aged*. This enlightens as to why there was no mention in the Bible of an image found on the Shroud at the time of Christ's resurrection. Even today, the image cannot be seen unless standing at least six to ten feet away from the

Shroud—any closer than that the image fades away into the straw-yellow background color of the cloth.

Biophysicist Dr. Jean-Baptiste Rinaudo (of the Center of Nuclear Medical Research in Montpellier, France, and of the Grenoble Nuclear Studies Center in France) developed the Protonic Model of Image Formation which demonstrates this. At the Grenoble Nuclear Studies Center, Dr. Rinaudo radiated proton beams onto white linens with a particle accelerator. The linens remained white until Dr. Rinaudo performed artificially induced aging on the linens. This gradually resulted in the same straw-yellow color found on the Shroud. In addition, only the outer most surfaces of the fibers were radiated and colored, the inner part of the fibers remained white—precisely matching this surprising characteristic discovered from the Shroud's fibers. Another effect of the proton radiation was how it replicated the Shroud's response to fluorescence. Linen fluoresces under ultraviolet light. The Shroud also fluoresces under ultraviolet light—but not where the image exists. The radiation experiments produced this same corresponding effect. Namely, wherever the particle radiation was applied to a linen cloth the fluorescent response also disappeared. Another important result of the radiation experiments is that *it also reproduced the identical molecular changes to the linen molecules, resulting in conjugated carbonyl (double bonded) molecular groups*, and after artificial aging, oxidized, dehydrated cellulose—*precisely what is found with the image fibers of the Shroud*. Dr. Rinaudo deduced that this evidence provided indication that a radiated image would begin to appear only gradually *after* a period of years. Dr. Kitty Little, retired nuclear physicist from Britain's Atomic Energy Research Establishment in Harwell, performed similar experiments with the same results.

From this understanding, we may now more precisely comprehend what a medieval forger from the 1300s must do in order to craft *this specific* Turin Shroud image. ***The medieval artisan must produce the*** *image* (not by applying paint or pigment to the Shroud) but, *by discharging particle radiation, and do so in a manner that:*

(1) *modifies the <u>molecular structure</u>(!) of the cloth's image area fibers (forming conjugated carbonyl, double-bonded groups),*
(2) *do so with a precision that rearranges the molecules to form a sharply focused photographic-like image (to be discovered four centuries later after the 1300s from the invention of photography in 1826),*
(3) *and simultaneously reconfigures the molecules to fashion its three-dimensional encodement.*

Six centuries after the medieval artist (late 20th century), scientists would develop the technology to discover and interpret this 3D molecular encodement. *A medieval craftsman would have to do all this without being able to see any effect of what he was trying to do to the Shroud* until years later when the Shroud began to age and yellow—revealing (at that time) only the blurry image seen by the natural eye. These three facts (listed above) are universally undisputed features of the Shroud. The only question is whether you think a medieval craftsman from the 1300s could have accomplished this.

(Note: If you informed a medieval craftsman from the 1300s that he must *ONLY* produce this Shroud image exclusively by *"modifying the molecules"* of the linen's fibers—*without applying any substance* upon the Shroud—his first question would be: *"What's a molecule?"* Have you ever seen a molecule with your naked, unaided eye? Neither could any medieval artist from the 1300s. And yet the medieval artist must engineer a restructuring of the linen image *molecules* so that *400 years later* (after the invention of photography in 1826) it would finally reveal its *photographic depiction*, and *600 years later* reveal its *three-dimensional image*. The medieval artist must accomplish this *exclusively by reconfiguring molecules* of the

Shroud cloth *(which molecules he CANNOT SEE, and DOES NOT KNOW EXIST)*!

Did a medieval craftsman accomplish this? Molecules were not proven to exist until 1926 when French chemist Jean Baptiste Perrin won the Nobel Prize in Physics for proving mathematically the existence of molecules. Even at that time molecules still could not be visually seen. Molecules were finally seen for the first time in year 2009 when IBM invented the first Atomic Force Microscope with a carbon monoxide tip. Scientists were not able to generate particle radiation until the late 20th century. Three-dimensional holography (to produce and view a 3D image) was not devised until Dennis Gabor originated its concept in 1947 and eventually won the 1971 Nobel Prize in Physics for the invention of the holographic method. In Chapter 8, we find documentation from peer-reviewed scientific papers that the Shroud *"is not explainable by Science nor reproducible up to now."* If international scientists of our modern times of technology still cannot reproduce the Shroud phenomenon, does it make sense that a medieval artisan from the 1300s could have accomplished this?

Chapter 7

FIRST CENTURY COINS FOUND OVER THE EYES?

Momentous discovery ensued one day while Ph.D. physicist John Jackson, together with Ph.D. Eric Jumper from the Dept. of Aeronautics and Astronautics, Air Force Institute of Technology, and Bill Mottern, image specialist at Sandia Laboratory were reviewing the three-dimensional image of the Shroud from the VP-8 Image Analyzer. They never would have noticed this discovery had it not been for the VP-8 analyzer. What caught their attention was something akin to three-dimensional buttons appearing over each eye of the Shroud victim.[f] What was this? Naturally, this roused the curiosity of researchers to more extensively scrutinize the matter. Professor Francis Filas of Chicago made the eventual discovery that these were apparent coins placed over the eyelids. Upon rigorous examination from Log E Interpretations Systems at Overland Park, Kansas, it was successfully demonstrated that the coins bore three-dimensional quality with embossed letters. The letters are about 1.5 millimeters high. Others later would confirm these findings. The coins were best apparent from enlarged photographs of the face made by film emphasizing contrast when the Shroud was stretched taut. It became evident that these buttons exhibited both letters and a symbol. Further research by Professor Filas discovered that the letters and the symbol matched lepton coins that were minted for Pontius Pilate between the years 29 and 32 (A.D./C.E.). (Pontius Pilate was the Roman Prefect [i.e., governor] of Judea who presided over the Roman trial and crucifixion of Christ.) The presence of the lepton coin characteristics was seen over both eyes, but was most clear from the coin over the right eye. An array of four letters ("UCAI") had remained on the coin. It was an abbreviation of the Greek inscription:

---

[f] Eventual experiments proved that a corona discharge from an embossed coin could produce this 3D effect.

"Of Tiberius Caesar" (TIBEPIO**UKAI**CAPOC). Some of these Pontius Pilate coins still exist today. However, numismatists had never noticed before (until observed on the Shroud) that the abbreviation was misspelled! The correct spelling should have been "UKAI" (instead of "UCAI" found on the Shroud). At first, some people insisted that the misspelling was evidence that the Shroud was a fraud. However, subsequent research identified several surviving Pontius Pilate coins still in existence bearing that exact misspelling ("UCAI"). (The error in minting was likely a phonetic misspelling because both spellings evoke the same hard "K" sound when pronouncing *"Caesar"* in Latin and *"Kaisaros"* in Greek.)

Another characteristic of the coin is that the letters appeared above a *lituus* symbol (an astrologer's staff with a handle arranged similar to a horizontally reversed/inverted question mark). The lituus symbol of the astrologer's staff was an official Roman government emblem found on *all* coins minted for Pontius Pilate from years 29 through 32 (A.D./C.E.). Pilate's usage of the lituus staff as his official Roman government emblem was unique within the Roman Empire. Since the reign of Pilate, the lituus symbol was never again used by any subsequent official throughout the history of the Roman Empire as an official government symbol.

The Roman date of the sixteenth year of the reign of Tiberius Caesar was found on the back of one of the surviving Pilate lepton coins. Arabic numbers did not yet exist at that time, so the coin bore Greek letters to indicate the date. There was an "L" (which signified that the following letters represented numbers), followed by "I" (used to denote a value of ten), followed by a Stigma letter (which looks like a rounded five and represents the number six). In summation, the surviving Pilate lepton coin was dating the coin as the *sixteenth year of the reign of Tiberius Caesar*, which would have been approximately 28-30 (A.D./C.E.). Unfortunately, the Shroud's image does not display that particular side of the coin. However, it is generally accepted that all Pontius Pilate coins bearing the lituus symbol were minted between 29-32 A.D./C.E.

This aspect of the Shroud (where coins appear over the eyelids) renders another instance of circumstantial evidence pointing toward identification of the Shroud victim. From this attribute, it would indicate that the Shroud victim was crucified sometime approximating 29-32 A.D./C.E. This was the same time frame when Christ was crucified. Furthermore, because the coins on the Shroud bore the unique official Roman lituus emblem of Pontius Pilate, this adds affirmation that the Shroud victim was crucified within the vicinity of the regional jurisdiction of the Roman Judean Prefect (governor) Pontius Pilate—who *personally* authorized the Roman crucifixion of Christ.

Some have suggested that the appearance of coins on the Shroud is only a coincidence of the weave patterns of the Shroud cloth. However, the following considerations argue against that:

(1) The coins would never have caught the attention of the scientists except that they protruded over each eye when viewing the three-dimensional image from the VP-8 Image Analyzer,

(2) The letters are precisely in the correct position relative to the lituus staff (a 9:00 to 11:30 position above the staff handle when the staff is viewed vertically).

(3) The letters are sequenced in the proper order.

(4) The letters are all aligned and facing in the proper direction (not upside down, sideways, at differing angles, or inverted).

(5) The shape and the facing direction of the curved hook on the lituus staff symbol matched the surviving Pilate coins.

(6) The ratio size of each characteristic relative to the size of the other characteristics, the size of the coin compared to

the body, the size of the letters compared to the lituus staff, and the shape of the coin (being clipped at the 1:30 to 3:30 clock position) matched the surviving Pilate lepton coins.

(7) The odds that the coin images should appear at this precise location on the Shroud (not just once, but twice — once over *each* eye) rather than at some other part of the 14'3" x 3'7" (or 4.34 m x 1.10 m) cloth are a factor.

(8) The mathematical probabilities of these various characteristics occurring by accident were calculated and found to be astronomical (one chance in eight million). This is a formidable mathematical argument against this aspect being a coincidental weave pattern of the Shroud cloth.

(9) Studies utilizing a polarized image-overlay technique identified some *74 points of congruence* between the Shroud coin and the Pilate lepton coins. It only requires 14 points of congruence to certify the identity of a fingerprint in a U.S. court of law. However, the Shroud had 74 points of congruence on the coin over the right eye and 73 over the left eye.

The ancient Jewish burial tradition of placing coins over the eyelids was not discovered until the final decades of the 20th century. Since then, many such archeological findings have been disinterred. Evidence indicates that the placement of coins over the eyes was a custom practiced within the vicinity of Jerusalem during the first century B.C./B.C. and the first century A.D./C.E. Considering that this Jewish burial tradition was not discovered until the late 20th century, how would a medieval forger think to include these features on the Shroud? How would the forger happen to obtain possession of a rare Roman Pontius Pilate coin (which during his medieval time was already 1,300 years old) to compare with and copy onto the Shroud?

Your appraisement regarding the apparent Pontius Pilate coin images over the Shroud eyelids: Is this most likely a concoction by a medieval counterfeiter? Or, could this be collateral evidence synchronized to the date, history, and location of Christ? (I.e., the *date*: coins dating *circa* 29-32 A.D./C.E.; the *history*: the historic Roman governor Pontius Pilate's official Roman lituus emblem on the coins, and the *location*: Pilate's regional jurisdiction of Judea).

From these coin features we find that there are more than just *unique* crucifixion wounds that point toward Christ as the Shroud's potential crucifixion victim (i.e., the unique crown of thorns, and the unique postmortem pierced side wound). Here, in this case, the Pontius Pilate coins now further point in the direction of Christ as the potential Shroud victim (i.e., via the date of such coins, the historical figure of Pilate, and the geographic region of Pilate's jurisdiction). Was this the hand of God orchestrating these clues?

Fig. 6.

Log E Interpretation photo of the Shroud's right eye area with a surving Pontius Pilate coin placed to the left of it.

Above is the apparent Pontius Pilate coin image from the Shroud's right eye area adjacent to a surviving Pontius Pilate coin on the left. The image was potentially produced by corona discharge that streamed off the elevated parts of the coin. The Greek letters **UCAI** (a reference denoting "of Tiberius Caesar") is displayed at the 11:00 position above the Pontius Pilate official Roman lituus symbol (an astrologer's staff which appears like a backward question mark). Some existing Pontius Pilate coins still exist with this image symbol and spelling. Such coins were minted for Pontius Pilate during 29-32 A.D./C.E. when he was the Roman Prefect (govenor) of Judea who authorized the crucifixion of Christ.

Fig. 7.

This sketch helps to visually locate the UCAI letters above the Pilate lituus staff symbol from the potential coin features that appear over the Shroud's right eye area (cf. fig 6 photo above).

There exists today surviving Pontius Pilate coins that bear the same spelling and lituus symbol.

Chapter 8

THREE RECENT SCIENTIFIC TEST RESULTS
FOR DATING THE AGE OF THE SHROUD CLOTH

In June, 2015, a scientific conference was convened at Padua University in Italy titled: "Workshop of Paduan Scientific Analysis on the Shroud." It announced the results obtained from Padua University in collaboration with five other European universities: Bologna, Modena, Parma, Udine, and Polytechnic of Bari pertaining to their latest scientific tests and findings of the Turin Shroud.

Summarizing their assessment of the original 1988 Carbon-14 tests of the Shroud, they reported:

> Regarding the TS [Turin Shroud] dating, **after the demonstration that the 1988 radiocarbon result is not statistically reliable, probably because of environmental pollution,** alternative dating methods based on chemical and mechanical tests showed that **its age is compatible with the period in which Jesus Christ lived in Palestine**. (Emphasis added) [g]

Among the peer reviewed scientific papers presented by the scientists were three new dating tests of the Shroud which employed modern dating methodologies more innovative than the thirty-year-old 1988 radiocarbon tests. The following abstract was written by professor Giulio Fanti (who has headed the Shroud Science Group consisting of about 140 scientists), Pierandrea Malfi, and Fabio Crosilla. In the

---

[g] *Introductory Paper: Scientific Results on the Turin Shroud Coming from a Paduan University Research Project,* Giulio Fanti, MATEC Web of Conferences 36 (2015) 00001, DOI: https://doi.org/10.1051/matecconf/20153600001, CC-BY-4.0 copyright license https://creativecommons.org/licenses/by/4.0/.

abstract of their peer reviewed papers, they summarized their findings as follows:

> The present paper discusses the results obtained using innovative dating methods based on the analysis of mechanical parameters . . . and of opto-chemical ones (FT-IR and Raman) . . . . [T]wo opto-chemical methods have been applied to test the linen fabric, obtaining a date of 250 BC by a FT-IR ATR analysis and a date of 30 AD by a Raman analysis. These two dates combined with the mechanical result, weighted through their estimated square uncertainty inverses, **give a final date of the Turin Shroud of 90 AD +/-200 years at 95% confidence level.** While this date is both compatible with the time in which Jesus Christ lived in Palestine and with very recent results based on numismatic dating, it is not compatible with the 1988 radiocarbon measurements . . . . (Emphasis added) [h]

The June, 2015 scientific conference hosted at the University of Padua, Italy, documented that the Shroud body image *"is not explainable by Science nor reproducible up to now"* (italics and emphasis added).[i] The Shroud has now withstood over forty years of international scientific scrutiny; and this is where we're at. If the sum of all scientific knowledge that exists in the world today, combined with all the modern-day technology available in the world today, and if after more than four decades of exhaustive scientific research it is *still impossible* for scientists to reproduce an image with all the

---

[h] Mechanical ond opto-chemical dating of the Turin Shroud, Guilio Fanti, Pierandrea Malfi and Fabio Crosilla, MATEC Web of Conferences, 36 (2015) 01001, DOI: https://doi.org/10.1051/matecconf/20153601001, CC-BY-4.0 copyright license https://creativecommons.org/licenses/by/4.0/.
[i] Giulo Fanti, *Introductory Paper: Scientific Results on the Turin Shroud Coming from a Paduan University Research Project,* MATEC Web of Conferences 36, 2015, Article 00001, DOI: https://doi.org/10.1051/matecconf/20153600001. Creative Commons License Attribution 4.0 International (CC by 4.0) https://creativecommons.org/licenses/by/4.0/.

characteristics found on the Shroud, how then could a medieval artist from the 1300s accomplish this?

Shroud science historian Mark Antonacci affirmed:

> [S]omething unique happened to the man in the Shroud that distributed *all* the **unfakable evidence** . . . . The extensive evidence on this cloth is not only consistent with, but also comprises *unforgeable* **evidence** of every aspect of the passion, crucifixion, death, burial and resurrection of the historical Jesus Christ. (Emphasis added) [j]

Many have wondered what sort of findings might have resulted had modern scientists been given an opportunity to scrutinize one of the reported miracles of Christ from the first century. Results documented here may offer just such an evaluation.

---

[j] Mark Antonacci, *Test the Shroud* (*n.p.*: Forefront Publishing Co., 2015), 277.

Chapter 9

HOW TO APPROPRIATE GOD'S REDEMPTION
TO OBTAIN ETERNAL LIFE
AND RESURRECTION AFTER DEATH

Pertaining to the eternal Kingdom of God, the Bible reports that "nothing impure will ever enter it . . . but *ONLY* those whose names are written in the **Lamb's book of life"** (Rev. 21:27 NIV, emphasis added). **How can we have our name "written in the Lamb's book of life"?** (Christ is often referred to in the Bible as the sacrificial "Lamb of God.") Remember: one day you will die. But Christ proclaimed the offer of a future resurrection with everlasting life, explained below.

It is important to consider the historic setting at the time of Christ. There was no such religion called Christianity at that time. Christ was presenting Himself as the Jewish Messiah to the people of Israel. The existence of Israel had its birth from the ancient Passover event in Egypt (1,500 years earlier). But now with Christ, God was revealing that this Savior was the promised Jewish Messiah. Furthermore, with the crucifixion of Christ occurring during the festival of the Jewish Passover in Israel, God was demonstrating that the ancient Passover in Egypt had been prophetic. Namely, it had pointed to a future event when Christ would become the ultimate Passover Lamb of God, sacrificed (crucified) to provide redemption (*not just for Israel, but now for the entire world*)! On the cross, the Messiah had borne God's judgment of the penalty of sin for all humanity. *Those who would place their faith in Christ's atonement for sin on the cross, and would make a commitment to dedicate their life to a devotion of loyalty to Christ,* they would receive forgiveness of sins, salvation from God's judgment of eternal wrath against sins, and would receive everlasting life in the future Kingdom of God. Their names would be written in "The Lamb's Book of Life."

Many people like to express this through prayer to God. We read, for example, that when Christ was crucified, two criminals were also crucified next to Him. One of them mocked Christ. But the other criminal rebuked the mocker—turning to the Nazarene, he implored from Christ: **"Remember me when You come into Your Kingdom"**! (Luke 23:42 TLV, emphasis added). Christ acknowledged and confirmed his request of faith right there on the cross! His name was written in the "Lamb's Book of Life."

According to the Bible, God must eventually judge sin to enforce righteousness. Since all of us have sinned, then according to the Bible everyone is in need of atonement for sin—no matter how good a person we may be. Consequently, we must either appropriate the atonement provided by Christ for our sins on the cross, or else we will have to bear our own eternal judgment from God for our sin. The Bible strongly affirms this. We need salvation and atonement. Otherwise, there is no reason why Christ would have to suffer and die for our sins. *This explains the purpose and significance of the suffering found on the Shroud. It is a centric feature of the Shroud's message.*

> In him [Christ] we have **redemption through his blood**, the forgiveness of sins . . . . (Eph. 1:7 NIV, emphasis added)

> God presented Christ as **a sacrifice of atonement**, through the shedding of his blood—**to be received by faith** (Rom. 3:25 NIV, emphasis added).

> You know that you were **redeemed** . . . not with perishable things . . . but **with the precious blood like that of a lamb** without defect or spot, **the blood of Messiah** (1 Peter 1:18 NIV, emphasis added).

Christ (who bore that tortured, brutal, crucifixion for our redemption), He is the One worthy to be revered. If you are willing,

He can guide you to fulfill His calling and unique mission for your life. Don't miss out on God's purpose for your life. Talk to Him—if not vocally, then from the silent depths of your soul and heart. He hears you. Bare your soul to Him. He knows you intimately . . . better than you know yourself. This is a personal commitment—a *mutual bond of devotion and loyalty—directly from Christ to you . . . and from you to Him.* If you humbly seek to follow Him, that opens the door for God to guide your life to fulfill His purpose and calling for your life. It is very precious to see God's hand of intervention in your personal life. You may not recognize it at the time, but looking back over your life, you may discover pieces of the puzzle that will begin to fit together. Even small things like offering a helping hand to others, or suffering that you may endure for the sake of Christ will all be rewarded by God in the resurrection (Mark 9:41).

> For we are **His workmanship**, created in Christ . . . **for good works, which God prepared beforehand that we should walk in them** (Ephesians 2:10 NJKV, emphasis added).
>
> Take heed that you do not do your charitable deeds before men, to be seen by them. Otherwise you have no reward from your Father in heaven. Therefore, when you do a charitable deed, do not sound a trumpet before you as the hypocrites do . . . that they may have glory from men. Assuredly, I [Christ] say to you, they have their reward. But when you do a charitable deed, do not let your left hand know what your right hand is doing, that your charitable deed may be in secret; and your Father who sees in secret will Himself reward you openly (Matthew 6:1-4 NKJV).

For those who are sincere about their commitment to Christ, they may demonstrate that sincerity by studying the Bible to learn what pleases God and what is disloyal to God. Christ taught that the Bible is *bread for the soul*—to **nurture us** and guide us in our relationship with God—and like a Father offering wise counsel to his cherished son:

He [Christ] answered and said, "It is written, *'Man shall not live by* **BREAD** *alone, but by every word [bread for the sole] that proceeds from the mouth of God'"* (Matt. 4:4 NKJV, emphasis added).

My son, if you receive my words, and treasure my commands . . . *and* apply your heart to understanding . . . then you will understand the fear of the LORD, and find the knowledge of God. For the LORD [like a father to his cherished son] gives wisdom; from His mouth *come* knowledge and understanding (Prov. 2:1-2, 5-6 NKJV, emphasis added).

[Christ] then said to those sectarian Jews who had believed him, "If you remain in my word, then you are truly my disciples. You will know the truth, and the truth will make you free" (Yoḥanan/John 8:31 MW).

"Come to Me, all *you* who labor and are heavy laden, and I [Christ] will give you rest. Take My yoke upon you and **learn from Me**, for I am gentle and lowly in heart, and you will find rest for your souls. For My yoke is easy and My burden is light." (Matt. 11:28-30 NKJV, emphasis added).

There is an excellent YouTube website with 321 videos where you can select and listen to any chapter of the entire Bible, clearly read, and simply explained—with fascinating insights from history, archeology, and science. You can read the Bible while listening. And you can also just enjoy listening while working in the kitchen or doing various chores around the house. To visit this website, type into any URL address bar (not into a search window) either: "**Chuck Smith – Bible Study – C2000 Series – from Genesis to Revelation**" or https://www.youtube.com/playlist?list=PLd5sqGfYOck6cwm-3uyEt45dHfs7CKcmP. To verify that you found the correct website, it must show selections for every chapter in the Bible. Then save that website to your favorites, or bookmark it for future quick and easy access.

(It is also fitting to attend a congregation where the Bible is taught and studied. There you will find further teaching, as well as a supportive bond within the family of God.)

Also, consider obtaining a copy of the complete book entitled: *The Turin Shroud: Physical Evidence of Life After Death? (With Insights from a Jewish Perspective)*. It reports far more extensive and compelling discoveries about the Shroud of Turin. It documents every fact with hundreds of reference notes. It also provides a riveting, rich, historical context from a Jewish perspective—transporting readers back into that authentic first century world at the time of Christ—with some surprising results.

Below is a sampling of some of the findings that scientists *unexpectedly* encountered pertaining to the ***identification of the Shroud victim***. You can read about all the details in the complete book. As a preview, the list below references a sample of some of the findings physically identified directly from the Shroud cloth by the scientists. They offer evidence toward identification of the Shroud victim:

- The image of the Shroud victim bears specific wounds of a crucified man. However, blood trails from the scalp, and a *post mortem* pierced side wound to the chest spilling blood with a gush of *water* were abnormal wounds—not typical of crucifixions. They correspond to Christ's unique crown cap of thorns (mocking him as the King of the Jews), and also to a specific **post mortem** pierce wound to Christ's chest **after** his death. The blood from the Shroud's chest also bares no sign of a pumping heart nor splattering from breathing—it was clearly a *post mortem* occurrence—the victim was already dead. It would be illogical to stab a crucified victim (shortening the intended torture)—and especially after he was already dead! Why do that? These unexpected anomalies point in direction toward Christ, rather than some random crucifixion victim.

Compare John 19:31-34 which documents the highly unusual circumstances that led to these unique wounds.

- [Pollen evidence]: Points to a specific geographical region of the world of the Shroud's origin (16-32 miles/10-20 km from East to West of Jerusalem).
- [Limestone]: Points to the geographical vicinity of Jerusalem.
- [Apparent coins over the eyes]: Date to a specific period of years (29-32 AD/CE)—matching when Christ was crucified.
- [Apparent coins over the eyes]: Evidence identifying the ruling governor (Pontius Pilate) at the time of the crucifixion.
- [Pollen]: Identifies a specific season of the year (March – April, i.e., the time of Passover) when Christ was crucified.
- [Floral images]: Point to the time of day (approximate hour of the day) when death occurred, matching the gospel narrative.
- [Body, and floral images]: Provide evidence indicating the duration of time that elapsed while the body/corpse was wrapped within the Shroud cloth (namely, two to three days).

How could such an old cloth provide attestation for such a wide variety of highly specific, unique details? Read the fascinating evidence in the complete, unabridged book—which includes many more surprising discoveries by the scientists: *The Turin Shroud: Physical Evidence of Life After Death? (With Insights from a Jewish Perspective)*.

Share the good news. Give some copies of this book to extended family, friends, and relatives. They may be interested to read for themselves about the scientific research exploring potential *physical evidence* of life after death.

> "The Shroud of Turin is the single, most studied artifact in human history" —*Journal of Research of the National Institute of Standards and Technology*, U.S. Department of Commerce.[k]

For God **so LOVED** the world **that He gave His only begotten Son,** that whosoever believes in Him should **not perish but have everlasting life. For God did not send His Son into the world to condemn the world, but that the world through Him might be saved** (John 3:16-17 NKJV, emphasis added).

This is the will of the Father who sent Me [Christ], that of all He has given Me I should lose nothing, but should **raise it up at the last day. And this is the will of Him who sent Me, that everyone who sees the Son and believes in Him may have everlasting life; and I will raise him up at the last day** (John 6:39-40 NKJV, emphasis added).

I know that my Redeemer lives, and at the last He will take His stand on the earth. **Even after my skin is destroyed, yet from my flesh I shall see God** (Job 19:25 NASB, emphasis added).

---

[k] Lloyd A. Currie, "The Remarkable Metrological History of Radiocarbon Dating [II]," *Journal of Research of the National Institute of Standards and Technology* 109, no. 2 (March-April 2004): 185-217, https://nvlpubs.nist.gov/nistpubs/jres/109/2/j92cur.pdf ; P. Damon, D. J. Donahue, B. H. Gore, A. L. Hatheway, A. J. T. Jull, T. W. Linick, P. J. Sercel, L. J. Toolin, C. R. Bronk, E. T. Hall, R. E. M. Hedges, R. Housley, I. A. Law, C. Perry, G. Bonani, S. Trumbore, W. Wölfli, J. C. Ambers, S. G. E. Bowman, M. N. Leese, and M. S. Tite, "Radiocarbon dating of the Shroud of Turin," *Nature* 337, (1989), 611-615.

For those who are persuaded that the Shroud is authentic:

- Did you ever think that someday you would be able to *see one of Christ's actual miracles from the first century?*
- Did you ever expect that one day you would *see Christ Himself with your own eyes during your lifetime?*
- Did you ever imagine that you would *personally witness the moment of Christ's resurrection?* (Which made the image.)
- *Selah* (Pause, and ponder . . . to appreciate this gift to you *provided <u>directly</u> from Christ Himself! – a bi-product of His resurrection . . .* and to see *His sufferings for your redemption.*)

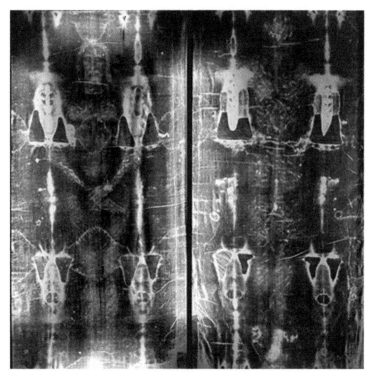

Fig. 4.

(For families that celebrate the observance of Easter or Passover, why not include a review of this book as part of your tradition . . . and to appreciate this special gift from Christ?)

MORE PHOTOS

National Geographic Magazine offers a wonderful gallery
of specially enhanced photos of the Shroud
which may be viewed from their feature article
"The Mystery of the Shroud"
at
http://home.kpn.nl/britso531/Nat.Geographic.June1980.pdf

PHOTO CREDITS

Regarding photos from Wikimedia Commons: Wikimedia Commons only utilizes images that are *not* subject to copyright restrictions (freely licensed, public domain, etc) which would not preclude anyone from using them for any purpose or at any time if the user adheres to the terms of the license. See the following URL for full details pertaining to this: Wikimedia Commons, "Commons Licensing," https://commons.wikimedia.org/wiki/Commons:Licensing.

Book cover photo   PD-Art I PD-old-100 I PD-1923 (Public Domain).
                       This is a faithful photographic reproduction of a two-
                       dimensional, public domain work of art. The work of art itself
                       is in the public domain for the following reason. This work is
                       in the public domain in its country of origin and other
                       countries and areas where the copyright term is the author's
                       life plus 100 years or less.
                       [Wikimedia Commons contributors, "File:Shroud of Turin
                       001.jpg," *Wikimedia Commons, the free media repository,*
                       https://commons.wikimedia.org/w/index.php?title=File:Shroud
                       _of_Turin_001.jpg&oldid=142378275 (accessed January 6,
                       2018).
                       (https://commons.wikimedia.org/wiki/File:Shroud_of_Turin_0
                       01.jpg)]

FIG. 1   PD-Art I PD-old-100 I PD-1923 (Public Domain).
                       This work is in the public domain in its country of origin and
                       other countries and areas where the copyright term is the
                       author's life plus 100 years or less.
                       [Wikimedia Commons contributors, "File:OntstaanLijkwade
                       GiovanniBattista.png," *Wikimedia Commons, the free media
                       repository,*
                       https://commons.wikimedia.org/w/index.php?title=File:Ontsta
                       anLijkwade_GiovanniBattista.png&oldid=273565822 (accessed
                       January 6, 2018).
                       (https://commons.wikimedia.org/wiki/File:OntstaanLijkwade_
                       GiovanniBattista.png)]

CPSIA information can be obtained
at www.ICGtesting.com
Printed in the USA
BVHW052141130522
637037BV00012B/66